P9-CDA-706

Hey You! C'mere

a poetry slam

by
Elizabeth Swados

illustrated by
Joe Cepeda

SCHOLASTIC INC.
New York Toronto London Auckland Sydney
Mexico City New Delhi Hong Kong Buenos Aires

Table of

Tough Kids	8
A Good Cry	10
Summer	13
Storm	16
Aunt Evelyn	18
Uh-Oh	21
Great Granma	23
Mr. Befuddled	24

Contents

The Telephone 27

Spaghetti 29

Silly Names 32

Monsters 34

Me 37

Sorry 42

Ice Cream 44

The Secret 46

Banging on a garbage can,
Bam bam bam.
Mattie says it's time
For a poetry slam.

Everybody's talkin' poems!

Everybody's laughin' poems!

Sis is eatin' poems!

Josh is drinkin' poems!

Amelia's wearin' poems on her feet!

The sky is filled with poems!

And Jacob rides a poem on the sidewalk

While Doria pours poems out of a pitcher.

Ratchit throws a poem at your back, ouch!

It's poem time, you have poems circling around your head,

You've got a poem in your pocket,
A poem on your tongue, did you know that?
You can be the poet and you can be the poem too.
Yesssss!

Tough Kids

"Hey you, c'mere,"
Says the kid down the street.
I hear his big mean feet.
"Hey you, c'mere,"
His voice is tough,
And his pushes are rough,
"Hey you, c'mere,
Whatsa matter witcha,
You sposta do what I
Tell ya to do.
I'll beatch ya if ya don't!"
I turn to him
With my sweetest grin,
And say,
"Hey you, guess what? I won't."

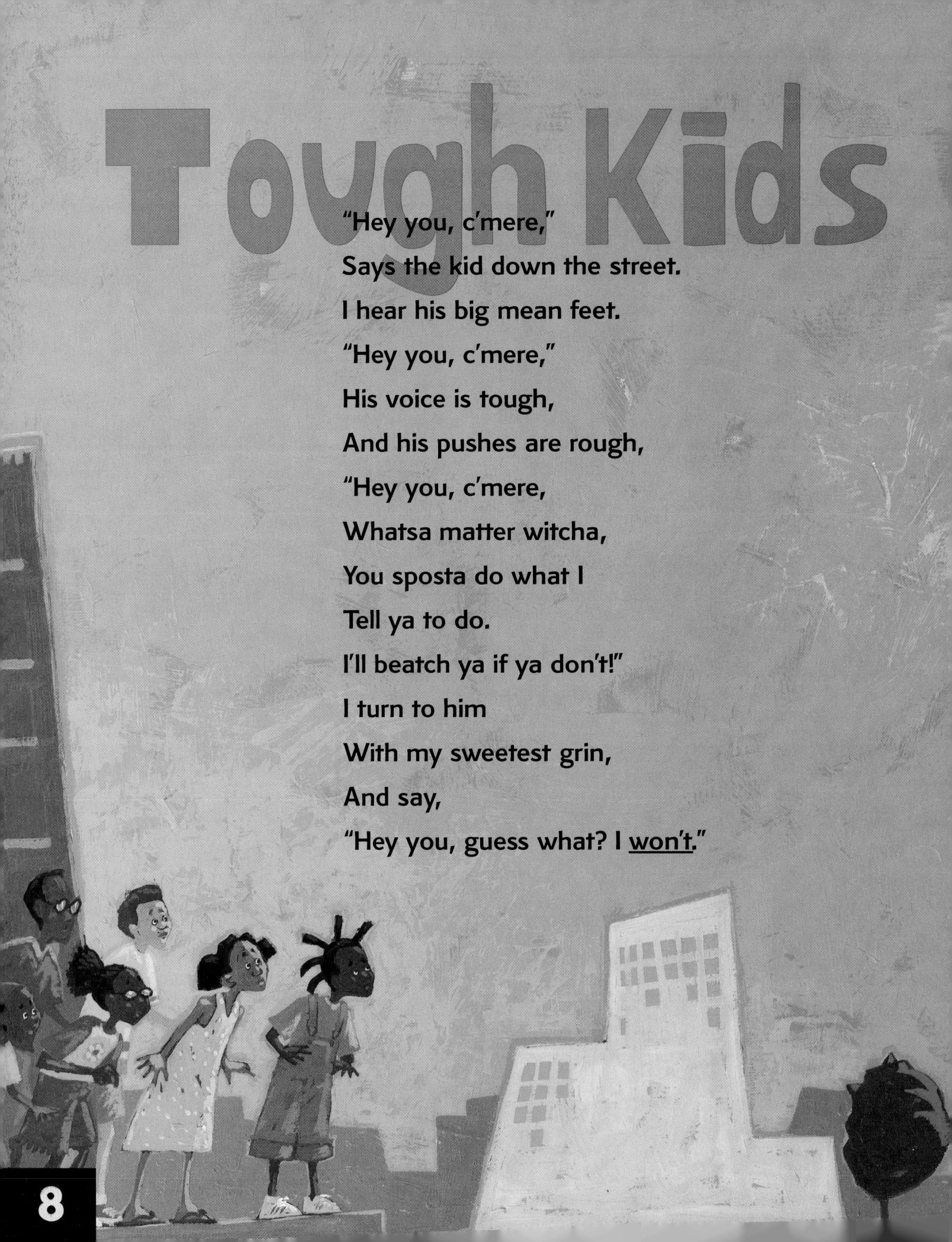

A Good

You may wonder why
But sometimes I like to cry.
I like the sound,
Haaw, haaw,
Wah, wah,
Eeee eee,
Hiccup cough sniff,
Hiccup cough sniff.
It's got a beat to it,
I like the taste of tear,
Lick, lick, lick.
Mom says, "What's the
matter, dear?"
Dad holds out his arms and says,
"Come here, come here."
It's not a bad deal,
Haaw wahee yaw,

Cry

To break down and howl,
To howl like a seal,
Aw aw aw aw,
To be like a bird and
Caw caw caw.
Crying can be really fun,
Except when you're hurt
or you're the one
Getting bopped.
Then it's like a waterfall,
And you can't stop.

But there's no time to cry, guys. Get into the summer mood.

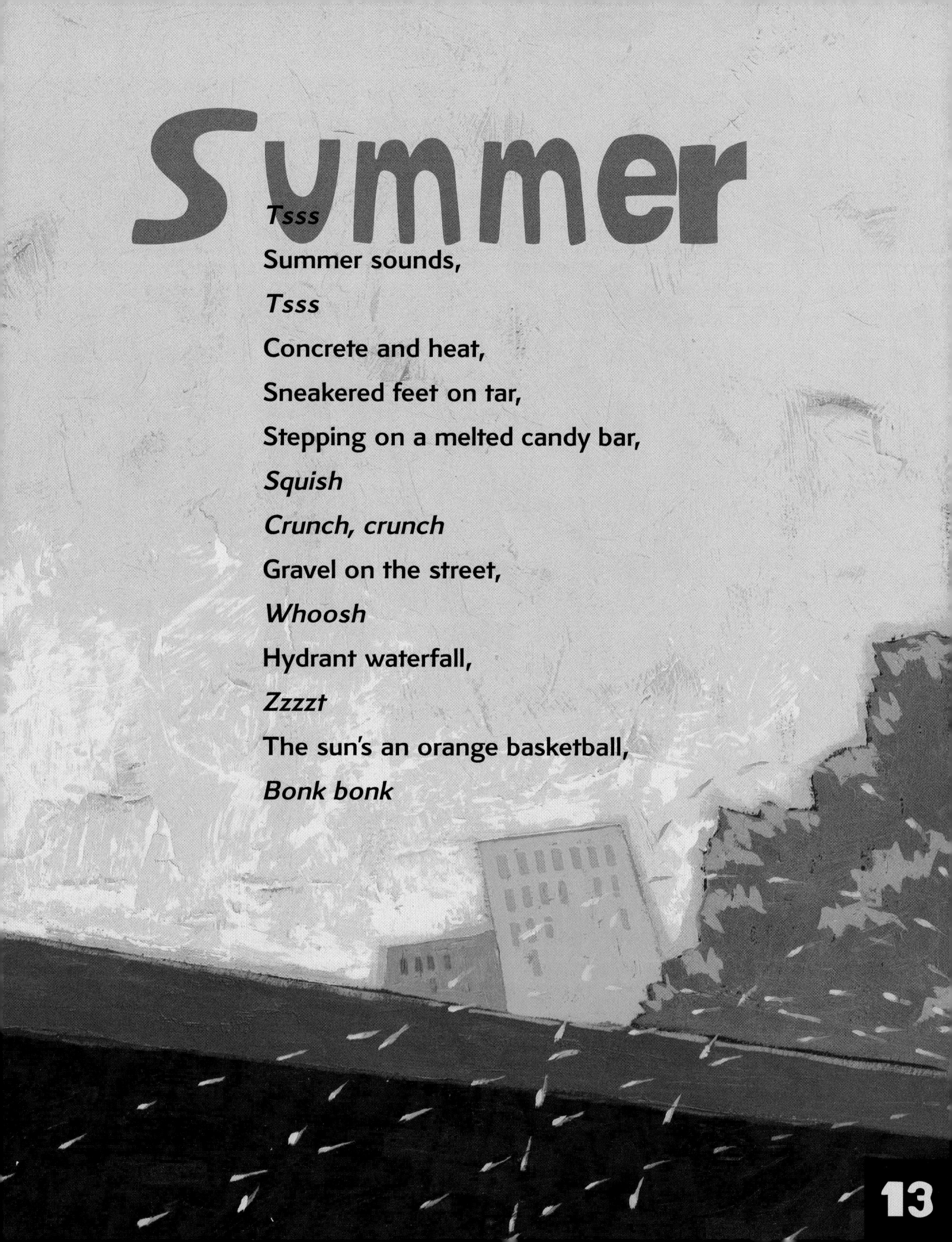

Summer

Tsss
Summer sounds,
Tsss
Concrete and heat,
Sneakered feet on tar,
Stepping on a melted candy bar,
Squish
Crunch, crunch
Gravel on the street,
Whoosh
Hydrant waterfall,
Zzzzt
The sun's an orange basketball,
Bonk bonk

Summer sounds,
And then the
Summer's gone.

Storm

Boom! Thunder!
Boom! Thunder!
First the lightning,
Crack!
It's frightening.
Then the ***BOOM***,
Thunder,
Outside my room.
BOOM, the thunder,
And the rain pours,
Like nails on the roof,
And ***POOF!***
Out go the lights.

What a night,
BOOM! Thunder!
Night of fright,
Night of wonder,
BOOM! Thunder.

Aunt
I'm going to kiss you,
Smooch you,
Koo-kootchie koo you.
I'm going to snuggle you,
Huggle you,
Niggle you and *nuggle* you,
Cuddle you too.
I'm going to pinch you,
Nuzzle you,
Fizzle you and *fuzzle* you.
Oh no! Not Aunt Evelyn!

Evelyn

Don't run away.
Oooh I could squeeze you,
Take a bite from your cute cheek,
Nibble all your fingers up,
And love you till you shriek.

Oh my sweet darling Daria.
Howdy doodle toodleoo.
Mmwwf!

Uh-Oh

Chomp chomp,
I'm naht suwposed to tawlk
Wid moy moudth fulled.
Chomp chomp,
Itds bayad mahnners.
Chomp chomp.

Here we are, but we're never gonna get in.
My Great Gramma
won't hear us.

Great Granma

Great Granma's kind of deaf – Ay?
Great Granma takes short breaths – oof
Great Granma's elbow creaks – eeh
Great Granma's eyes can leak – yuk
Great Granma laughs with a wheeze – hyee
Great Granma gets mad when you tease – DANG
Great Granma sometimes mumbles – mmm
Great Granma sings through her nose – nana
Great Granma likes to doze – zzz
Great Granma sometimes forgets – Who?
Great Granma has not one regret – NO SIR!
Great Granma likes to tell stories – Blah blah
Sometimes her stories are boring – zzz
Great Granma loves everyone – Bless you all
She calls us her daughters and sons – My you're tall!
Great Granma's as good as they get – Hooray!
Great Granma has not one regret – NO SIR!

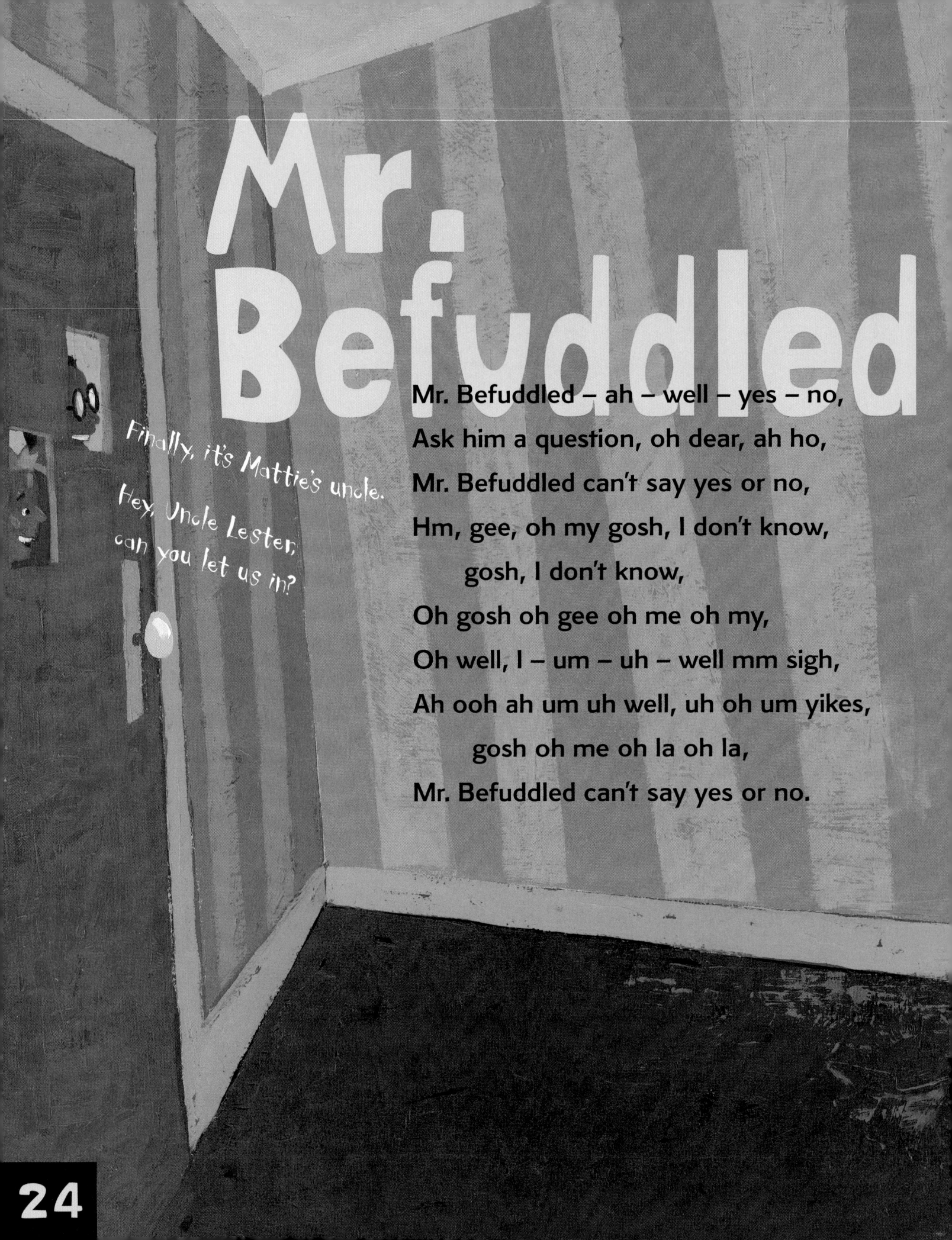

Mr. Befuddled

Finally, it's Mattie's uncle.

Hey, Uncle Lester, can you let us in?

Mr. Befuddled – ah – well – yes – no,
Ask him a question, oh dear, ah ho,
Mr. Befuddled can't say yes or no,
Hm, gee, oh my gosh, I don't know,
gosh, I don't know,
Oh gosh oh gee oh me oh my,
Oh well, I – um – uh – well mm sigh,
Ah ooh ah um uh well, uh oh um yikes,
gosh oh me oh la oh la,
Mr. Befuddled can't say yes or no.

The Tele

Mom, I brought the poets home!
If she's like my mom she'll never hear you!

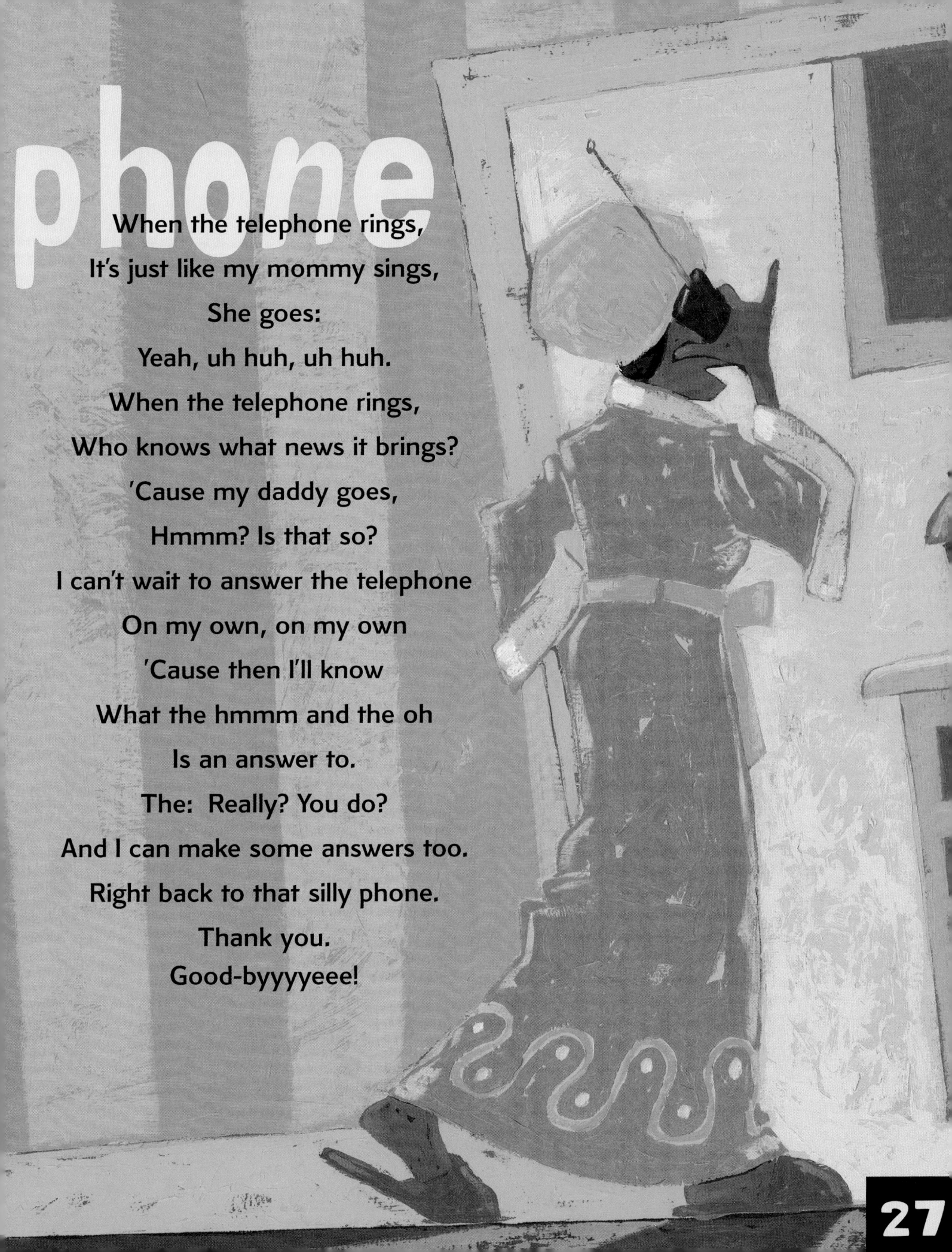

phone

When the telephone rings,
It's just like my mommy sings,
She goes:
Yeah, uh huh, uh huh.
When the telephone rings,
Who knows what news it brings?
'Cause my daddy goes,
Hmmm? Is that so?
I can't wait to answer the telephone
On my own, on my own
'Cause then I'll know
What the hmmm and the oh
Is an answer to.
The: Really? You do?
And I can make some answers too.
Right back to that silly phone.
Thank you.
Good-byyyyeee!

Mmm, what's cooking?
Poetry gives me an appetite.

Spaghetti

Schlump one long piece of spaghetti,
I'm gonna get it, yep I'm ready,
Breathe in deep,
Here I go,
Schlurp, schlurp, schlurp, schlurp,
Oh no,
How long does this spaghetti grow?
This one piece just goes and goes,
Schlurp, schlurp, schlurp, schlurp,
Schlurp, schlurp, schlurp, schlurp,

It's wrapped around my elbows,
It's tangled in my toes,
It doesn't seem to stop,
It's going up my nose,
I'm covered with meat sauce,
I better take a bath,
That's the longest piece of spaghetti
I've ever, ever,
Ever, ever
Had.

Silly
One of my favorite games
Is making up silly names
Mr. Grub T. Mudstuck, Diane Doobey Doo,
Fineas Figmuff and Tina Tutoo,
Teacup O'Hara, Tushi O'Lay,
Flutfarf, Zegba, and Snarky McKay,
Flubba Dubba Zinga Dinga,
Harken, Larken Sputzey Fritter,
I'm spaghettied out. Let's play a game —
the dumbest game I know.

Names

Bubby and Tubby Zarcofsky,
Pudding Blatt Bearallapopsky,
Mr. and Mrs. Blurpglopyahoo,
Grinspok, Jijigern, Yuggle Face Magoo,
And if these names aren't silly enough for you,
Make some yourself,
you *blubba checkoo.*

Monsters

I've checked the inside of my closet,
I've searched under my bed,
I don't know where that *ooh ooh*
Comes from,
Is that the sound of the dead?
Ooh Ooh Ooh Ooh
What a low, sad cry,
It could be the wind in the trees,
But why does it sound like a ghostly sigh?
Ooh Ooh Ooh Ooh
And sometimes *Ee ee ee,*

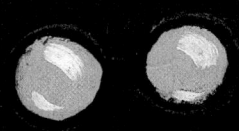

Wait—stop—shhh.

What's that howl?

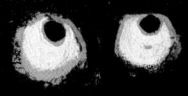

oooooooooooooooooooooooooooooooooooooooooooooooooohhhhhhhh

Is there a spirit flying around
And is it calling me?
If only it weren't so dark in here,
I could meet it face-to-face,
I'd say, "Come on, stop haunting me,
Go and find your own dang space!"
But I'm supposed to be in bed,
And I hear that mournful cry,
Ooh Ooh Ooh Ooh
Someone's crying
And I don't know why.

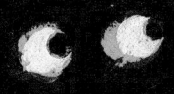

I'm so scared . . .

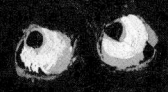

What's that crash?

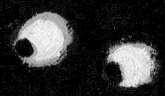

hhhh

Ha! Ha! Guess who?
I pulled another brilliant prank on you!
What a bully!

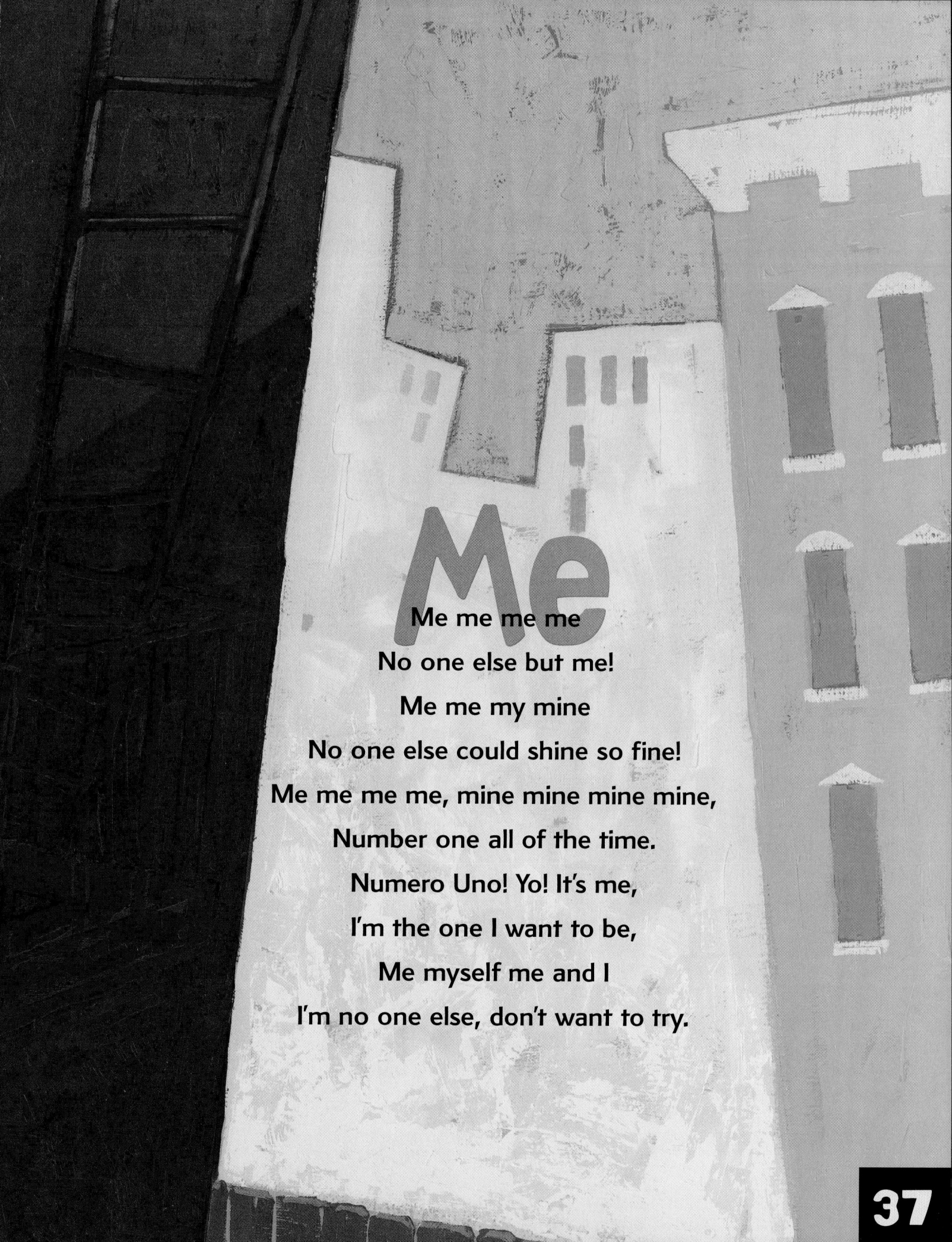

Me

Me me me me
No one else but me!
Me me my mine
No one else could shine so fine!
Me me me me, mine mine mine mine,
Number one all of the time.
Numero Uno! Yo! It's me,
I'm the one I want to be,
Me myself me and I
I'm no one else, don't want to try.

First of first, most of most,
I'm myself and I don't boast,
Me me now and me me then,
Me myself and me again,
I'm myself and I don't boast,
Me to me from coast to coast.

Group: Hey you, c'mere.

Mattie: Why you give us a rough time? We're gonna get you back with rhythm and rhymin'.

Josh: We wouldn't pay a dime to see your show of tough stuff.

Group: It's enough!

Amelia: You sneak up on us. You think we're weak?

Doria: Hey, we got camaraderie and poetry and you are the freak show.

Jacob: Who won't share his words
and his stories with us.

Group: It's your loss.

Mattie: That's da cost. Hey, you can
shake yo' fist.

Jacob: But scarin' us is history.

Sis: We're bigger—we've grown.

Amelia: Whereas you—

Group: Hey you, over dere. You're alone.

Ratchit: Uh . . . uh . . . oh . . . my . . .

But we've got each other.
What have you got?

Sorry

I'm sorry sorry sorry.
So sorry oh so very sorry,
Very very sorry, so very very sorry,
So sad and sorry sad and sorry sorry,
Oh so sad and oh so sorry very very sad,
And very very sorry I was so stupid and
Now I'm stupid sad and sorry, stupid sorry
Sad and very sorry, sorry sorry. It was stupid
And I'm sorry, so very sad and very sorry,
I was selfish and stupid
And I am so sorry oh so
Very very sad and sorry for
Being selfish and stupid. I'm sad.
And sorry. I'm sorry.

ICE CR AM

Ice Cre

I got some ice cream,
Slurp, slurp, slurp,
All around my tongue,
Lick, lick, lick,
Gotta beat the sun,
Slurp, slurp, slurp,
Or it'll drip,
Lick, lick, lick,
Here comes my dog,
Slurp, slurp, slurp,
Gotta give her some,
Lick, lick, lick,
Look at her tongue,
Lick, lick, lick,
So pink and slick,
Drip, drip, drip,
Now it's almost gone,
Slurp, slurp, slurp,
Right down to the cone,
Crunch, crunch, crunch,

Don't wanna miss a drop,
Drip, drip, drip,
I'll lick till there's none,
Crunch, slurp, drip, crunch, gone.

The Secret

Psst psst

I've got a little secret,

I want to tell you,

Psst psst

Shhh shhh

I love you,

I do,

I do,

I *doo doo doo bee doo*

Do!

Time for good-bye poems.
See you tomorrow poems.
Don't forget!
The end.